Exploring Shipwrecks

Exploring the fascinating mysteries of the deep blue sea

Nigel Marsh

young reed

Contents

Introduction

Shipwreck – that one simple word that makes you think of sunken treasure, pirates, Spanish galleons, pieces of eight or gold doubloons. Unfortunately, the vast majority of ships that sink never carried gold, silver or anything else of great value. The real treasure of most shipwrecks is their fascinating history and how exciting they are to explore when they end up on the ocean floor.

Exploring shipwrecks is something everyone can do. While many ships sink in deep water, others settle in shallow water and can be explored by scuba divers and snorkelers. Some shipwrecks even end up on land, so you can explore them without getting wet.

One of the reasons that shipwrecks are so interesting to explore is that they completely change once under the sea. When they end up on the bottom of the sea floor they become artificial reefs, covered in sponges, corals and other growth. This transforms a ship's bare hull into a living reef. Shipwrecks also attract marine life like a magnet, so become home to a wide variety of marine creatures.

In this book, you will explore a fascinating range of shipwrecks and discover how they ended up sinking. Some of the wrecks sunk under tragic circumstances, while others were scuttled for divers to enjoy. So let's submerge and explore the amazing world of shipwrecks.

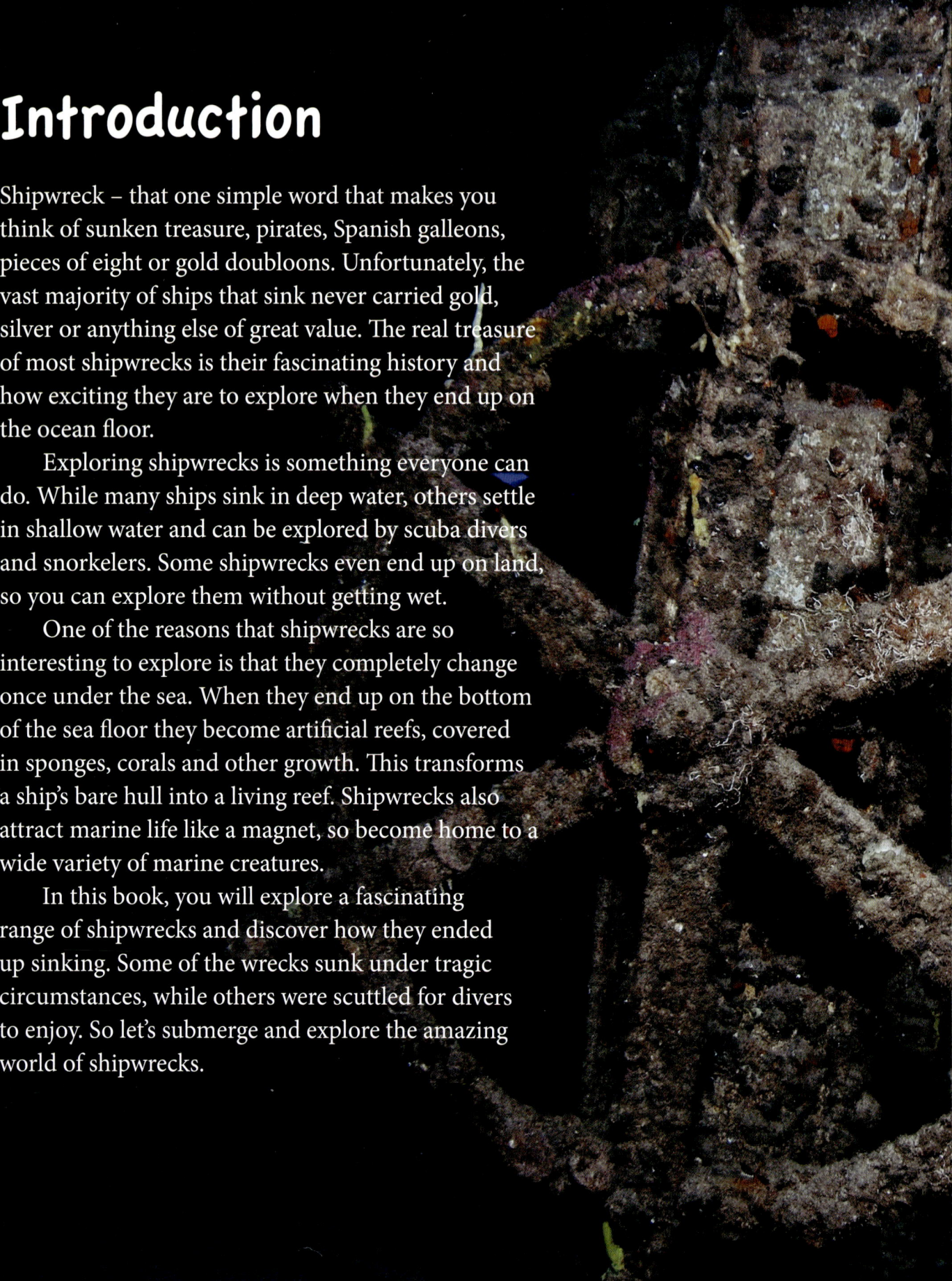

How Do Ships Sink?

Ships sink in a variety of ways and for a great number of reasons. Of course, when any ship sinks it is a great tragedy, as it can involve the loss of human lives.

Rough weather, caused by cyclones, typhoons and hurricanes, has been the cause of countless sunken ships. Rough weather causes shipwrecks when huge waves result in the ship capsizing, filling with water or snapping in half.

Ships also sink when they run into objects like coral reefs, submerged rocks, whales, other ships and even icebergs.

Many ships have sunk because their cargo is not secured properly, and when the ship is faced with heavy seas, it moves and causes the ship to roll over.

Ships often sink during wars. Throughout World War II thousands upon thousands of ships were lost during battle due to underwater mines, bombs dropped by planes or torpedos fired by submarines.

But not all ships sink due to unforeseen circumstances. Some ships are deliberately scuttled because they have outlived their usefulness. In times past these old ships were sunk in deep water, just to be rid of them, but today many of these ships are sunk as artificial reefs and become diving and fishing attractions.

Even with advances in technology, like radar and GPS, many ships still tragically sink each year and become shipwrecks.

The former navy warship HMAS Brisbane, being scuttled off Australia.

Did you know that some ships can change names many times over their lifetime, especially when they change ownership? Many sailors believe it is bad luck to change a ship's name and some will refuse to work on these ships. Some believe that the change of name is the cause for the sinking of a ship.

What Happens When A Ship Sinks?

When a ship sinks, it is often a disaster. People can drown, cargo can be lost and the ship's fuel or cargo can pollute the environment.

   The most immediate action when a ship sinks is to save the passengers and crew. These people are rescued from the sinking ship, lifeboats or directly from the water, by other ships or helicopters that arrive at the scene.

Did you know that the most expensive environmental disaster resulting from a shipwreck happened in 2002 when the oil tanker *Prestige* sank off Spain? It cost 2.8 billion dollars to clean up the mess.

(Main photo) The *MV Union Star 17* shipwreck, which sank off Malaysia in 2000.

Once all the people are safe, the next major concern is oil that could pollute beaches, kill seabirds and other marine life. Containing the oil can be a major problem, especially if the wreck has occurred in rough seas. The oil will generally be transferred to another ship, but if it cannot be contained it can cost millions of dollars to clean up afterwards.

All ships and cargo are insured, and when a ship sinks, it goes through an insurance assessment to determine its fate. Can the ship be refloated? Can the ship or parts of the ship be salvaged? Can the cargo be saved? Is the ship a complete loss?

Salvaging a ship is a very difficult process and will depend on how deep the ship has sunk and how badly broken up it is. Salvaging a ship can take months or even years. Occasionally the entire ship can be refloated, but more often it may need to be cut into sections to be raised. If deemed unsalvageable, the ship will be left on the sea floor – left to be taken over by marine life.

The Transformation Of A Ship Into A Reef

When a ship sinks it changes by the sea in a number of ways. Ships that run aground on rocky coastlines are quickly broken up by the powerful action of waves. Ships that end up on sandy beaches can remain intact for many years, only to slowly crumble as they rust or rot. However, it is ships that end up fully submerged that go through the most dramatic change.

While timber ships usually break up over time, steel ships are not so fragile and will stay intact and undergo an amazing transformation. The ship's once bare hull becomes coated in algae within days. The shipwreck then starts to morph into something completely different, a living reef.

In cooler temperate waters sponges and kelp start to grow on the hull. In warmer tropical seas lovely corals begin to appear. Within a few years the ship will become something new, as it transforms into an amazing living reef; and home to a wide range of marine life.

Did you know that shipwrecks are used by research scientists to study the growth rates of corals? Ships sunk as artificial reefs are perfect for this research as the date they are scuttled is documented allowing the scientists to know how long it took the corals to establish and grow.

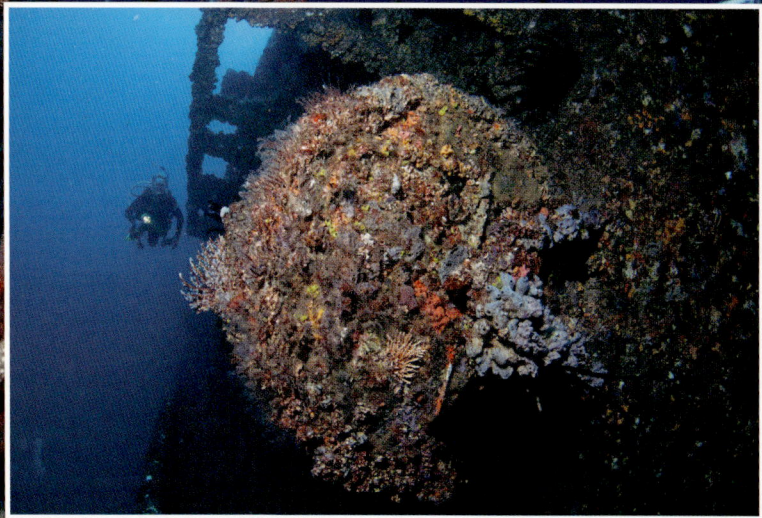

After five years underwater this hose reel on *HMAS Brisbane* was completely covered in marine growth.

(Main photo) Corals grow all over the *SS Yongala* shipwreck, Australia.

Marine Life Magnet

When a ship sinks and becomes an artificial reef, it soon attracts an incredible amount of marine life.

Small fish quickly find shipwrecks. How they find the new addition to the sea floor is completely unknown. Shipwrecks have many nooks and crannies, and to a fish, they are a perfect home, with plenty of places to hide from larger fish that might otherwise eat them.

Invertebrate species also quickly populate shipwrecks, with barnacles one of the first creatures to appear. When barnacles are in their larval stage, they drift with ocean currents and attach to any bare surface. A shipwreck provides a perfect surface to establish a home. They are quickly followed by crabs, shrimps and molluscs like mussels, octopus, squid and cuttlefish. Starfish are also attracted to shipwrecks, as are their close relatives the featherstars, sea urchins and sea cucumbers.

Shipwrecks also attract reef fish and schools of baitfish seeking shelter. Larger pelagic fish like barracuda, trevally and mackerel soon follow, attracted by the smaller fish that make for a tasty meal. Finally larger creatures like stingrays, turtles, gropers and sharks arrive.

In only a matter of years a once barren ship becomes an incredible marine ecosystem.

Did you know that Queensland gropers, the largest of all the gropers, are more commonly seen on shipwrecks than on their natural reef habitat? These gropers love to shelter in caves, and have found that shipwrecks offer them more hiding holes than most reefs.

(Main photo) Schools of goatfish and grunts on a shipwreck off Mexico.

Schools of grunts cover a shipwreck off Mexico.

Thousands of fusiliers on a shipwreck off Australia.

Queensland groper.

Creating An Artificial Reef

When ships are deliberately sunk to make artificial reefs for divers to enjoy, there is a lot of work that needs to be done to make them safe for both the marine environment and divers.

All the fuel is removed and the fuel tanks are thoroughly scrubbed. The oil used to power the ship's engine is very harmful to the marine environment. Other toxins and harmful substances, like asbestos, are also removed and disposed of carefully.

Electrical cabling and wires are stripped out of the ship as they could come loose and entangle a diver exploring the wreck. Another hazard to divers are doors and hatches, which could accidently close and entrap a diver. Therefore, doors and hatches are either removed or welded shut.

One of the biggest jobs when preparing a ship to be scuttled is the removal of the anti-foul paint, which is painted on the hull below the waterline to stop algae and barnacles attaching to the ship and slowing them down. This anti-foul paint is scraped off to allow marine life to grow all over the hull.

Access holes are cut into the side of the ship to allow divers to safely enter the ship and explore, while also allowing daylight to reach into the darker parts of the ship's interior.

The cleaning and preparation process can take up to a year and cost around one million dollars. But this is money well spent as purpose sunk shipwrecks attract many thousands of divers each year, pouring millions of dollars into the local economy.

Once the ship is cleaned it is towed to the site where it will be sunk. A sandy sea floor is the preferred location as sinking the ship on a rocky bottom can cause the ship to break up. Explosives experts then set charges below the waterline. Once detonated, the ship fills with water and sinks in only a few minutes. If all goes well the ship settles on the bottom sitting upright on its keel, and is now ready for divers to explore.

HMAS Brisbane, one of Australia's most famous artificial reefs.

Did you know that many navy ships have recycled names? One of Australia's most popular artificial reefs, *HMAS Brisbane* (featured on page 42) was the second warship to carry that name, the first was a light cruiser, launched in 1915 and decommissioned in 1935.

Finding Old Shipwrecks

Many millions of ships have been lost at sea since humans first started to use ships as a form of transport thousands of years ago. While the locations of some shipwrecks are well known, the great majority of ships disappear in the vastness of the oceans and are never seen again, unless someone is prepared to search for them.

Finding shipwrecks is what some 'wreck hunters' love to do. The search generally starts in a library, reviewing shipping records, reports from survivors, captain's logbooks or the journal of someone that visited the wreck site. The older the ship, the more difficult this search will be and it may take many years to find enough information to locate the general area where the ship disappeared.

Once a search area is pinpointed, the expensive work of locating the exact shipwreck site is undertaken. This generally involves the use of a magnetometer, a device dragged behind a ship that detects metal on the sea floor. But for more complicated searches, it might also involve the use of side-scanning sonar, remotely operated vehicles and other sophisticated equipment. But there is never any guarantee of success.

One of the most famous shipwrecks of all is the *RMS Titanic*, which sank in 1912 after striking an iceberg. It took dozens of search teams many years to find the elusive ship, which was finally found in 1985, 4km (2.5 miles) below the ocean surface.

People search for lost shipwrecks for many different reasons. For some, it is the quest for treasure. For others it is important to find the ship to discover why it sank or so the relatives of those lost will know where their loved ones rest. Other wreck hunters search for shipwrecks just for the joy of being the first to explore a new shipwreck.

Did you know the oldest shipwreck in Australia so far discovered is the British ship *Trail*? This ship ran into a reef off Western Australia and sank in 1622. Its crew were probably the first Englishmen to set foot on Australian soil, almost 150 years before Captain Cook arrived in 1770.

While more recent steel ships can remain intact for 100 years (above), older timber ships become completely broken up once they sink (main photo).

Salvaging A Shipwreck

Removing cargo and other items off a shipwreck is not an easy task, and salvage techniques and technology has changed greatly over the years.

In ancient times free divers, only descending on a single breath of air, were used to salvage the cargo off sunken ships. The amount of cargo that could be brought to the surface depended on how deep the shipwreck was and how good the free divers were. The best of these free divers could probably reach a depth of 30m (98ft), but most of this salvage work would have been done on ships that were in water less than 15m (49ft) deep. This technique was used for thousands of years until more creative inventions came along, some more successful than others.

The first of these inventions was the diving helmet, which came into use in the 15th century. These helmets could only be used in very shallow water and were often very dangerous, drowning many divers.

The next big step in shipwreck salvage came in the 17th century when the diving bell was invented. This was like an inverted drum that could be lowered to the sea floor with a diver inside in a large air pocket. The diver could then swim out and tie a rope to an item to be recovered, before returning to the air pocket in the diving bell.

However, the diving bell had limited uses and was quickly forgotten when a better diving helmet was developed in the 1830s. With air pumped from the surface, the new diving helmet allowed a diver to stay submerged for longer periods of time. This new diving helmet showed its worth when a diver salvaged 28 cannons off the *Royal George* shipwreck, off England, in 1834.

However, divers using these early model diving helmets had to be very careful. They were very heavy and not sealed at the bottom, and if tipped over would fill with water. Not long after this, someone had the smart idea to connect the helmet

Did you know the deepest salvage to date was not on a shipwreck, but on a plane? In 1987 a South African Airways flight crashed off Mauritius, with its flight data recorder recovered from a depth of 4.9km (3 miles).

to a suit that would keep the diver dry and allow them to work to depths of 60m (196ft) or more. This became known as the standard dress diving suit, and these suits are still used today, but they have become much more sophisticated and lightweight.

Diving to great depths exposes salvage divers to many dangers. The greatest being the bends or decompression sickness. The bends occurs when tiny bubbles of nitrogen enter the blood stream and expand, causing terrible pain or even death.

With the invention of SCUBA in the 1940s, this became the main type of equipment used by divers to salvage shipwrecks in depths no deeper than 60m (196ft). But for deeper shipwrecks divers still use more advanced standard dress diving gear, using mixed gases that allows them to work to depths of almost 200m (656ft).

Over the years, other salvage techniques have come and gone, and more recently remotely operated vehicles have been used to successfully salvage shipwrecks in water so deep that a diver could never reach.

Salvage work is not an easy operation and it can be very dangerous. Divers have to work in tough conditions, which could include deep, dark, dirty and cold water. It would be nice if all ships sank in clear, shallow and warm water, but many ships sink in harbors and rivers that are usually very murky. Sometimes the water is so murky that the divers can only work by feel. Salvage divers get paid a lot of money for the work they do, but it is very dangerous work.

(Left) Modern dive suit.

(Right) Old standard dress dive suit.

Treasure Shipwrecks

Every diver dreams of finding a treasure laden shipwreck. This has happened to a few very lucky divers who have stumbled across an undiscovered shipwreck. Generally though, to find a treasure ship you have to do a lot of research and spend a lot of money.

The ancient Greeks, Romans and Egyptians all used ships to move cargo, for transport and during warfare. They, and many other ancient cultures, all lost ships at sea. If lost in shallow water these ships were salvaged by free divers. However, if they sunk in water too deep for a free diver to reach, they were quickly forgotten.

In modern times these ancient shipwrecks started to be rediscovered when scuba divers first explored the oceans. While some of these ships were found to contain gold and other valuable items, their real worth was of an archaeological nature, as they provide a precious snapshot of ancient times. Found on these shipwrecks have been amphora, used to store wine or olive oil, sculptures in stone or bronze, coins, pottery and items of war such as swords, shields, helmets and daggers.

Almost all the ancient cultures of the world used ships, and each time an old shipwreck is discovered it reveals a little more about how these people lived and worked.

Some of the most famous treasure ships ever lost at sea were the Spanish galleons of the 16th and 17th century. During this time, many European nations were exploring the new world and establishing colonies in distant lands, and it was the Spanish that had the richest colonies in

Did you know that the people that discover treasure shipwrecks often don't get any of the treasure? All shipwrecks are either owned by someone or claimed by governments. So finding a treasure ship might make someone else very rich.

Mexico and regions of South America. After plundering the gold, silver and gems of these nations, they would send them back to Spain on ships, many of which were lost to pirates, uncharted reefs or in stormy seas.

One of the richest Spanish galleon shipwrecks so far discovered is the *Nuestra Senora de Atocha*, which sank off Florida, USA, in 1622. Rediscovered in 1985, after a 17 year search, the treasure on this ship is worth 450 million dollars.

But treasure doesn't always have to be gold or silver. The Chinese treasure ships found in the waters of Southeast Asia are full of priceless porcelain. Sailing from China to ports across Asia for centuries, these junks, as the Chinese ships are known, often sank with their holds full of porcelain bowls, plates and figurines.

More recent treasure shipwrecks of the last century have included ships lost during World War II that were carrying bullion of either gold or silver to pay for supplies. One of these ships was the British steam ship *SS Garisoppa*, which was torpedoed by a German U-boat (submarine) in 1941 and sank off the coast of Ireland. Rediscovered in 2011 at a depth of 4.7km (3 miles), a team working at great depth salvaged its cargo of silver, reported to be worth 200 million dollars.

While many treasure shipwrecks have been found, there are many more treasure shipwrecks that are awaiting discovery.

Maritime Archaeology

Archaeology on land is well documented, with archaeologists excavating sites in Egypt, Greece and many other countries to study our ancestors and their ancient culture. However, archaeologists also work underwater and study shipwrecks in much the same manner as they would an ancient building on land.

Did you know that many old shipwrecks around Australia are protected as historic sites? They are listed to stop divers removing items off the shipwreck, whether the item is valuable or not.

Studying a shipwreck underwater is quite a challenge for an archaeologist. Not only can the sea be rough and the water dirty, but tides, currents and the depth of water can also limit the amount of time they can spend on the wreck site. But why do archaeologists study shipwrecks?

A shipwreck, no matter how old, is like a giant time capsule, a reflection on the people and their culture at that time. By studying shipwrecks archaeologists can learn how the ship was built, the ship's layout, what cargo it was carrying and even what the crew were like.

Like on land, maritime archaeology can involve a lot of digging, as many old timber ships break up and get buried by sand. Once the shipwreck site is identified the archaeologist will set up a grid, so that the position of all items recovered can be accurately documented. A photo-mosaic of the site is also taken, with hundreds of pictures stitched together like a giant map of the shipwreck.

Removing the sand off a shipwreck is done using a large suction hose that pumps the sand away from the wreck. It can be a long process to remove metres of sand, but without the covering of sand the ship would not have been preserved. Timber, fragile metals and even paper can be preserved under sand, but once excavated it requires complex treatments to preserve these items. It can take many years for a team of archaeologists to excavate and study a shipwreck, but what they learn gives us all a better understanding into how our ancestors lived.

Maritime archaeologists explore an old timber shipwreck.

Exploring Shipwrecks

What lures divers and snorkelers to explore shipwrecks? Shipwrecks are fascinating to explore, and completely different to diving on a coral reef. Seeing what was once a mighty ship lying on the bottom of the ocean is always a breathtaking sight, and being able to investigate cabins, engine rooms and passageways where people once walked or worked is a unique experience.

For anyone interested in history, shipwrecks are a time capsule, as you are diving a part of history that maybe ten, 50, 100 or one thousand years old. Once you know the history of a shipwreck; where it was built, how it was built, what voyages it undertook, what people it carried, how it sunk, what happened to the survivors, what battles in was involved in and what ships it might have sunk – then you are really starting to get wreck fever, and appreciate the hidden world of shipwrecks.

Others that are not particularly interested in rusty metal or history still enjoy exploring shipwrecks as they are a haven for marine life. Many shipwrecks have more marine species on them than nearby reefs, especially the ones that rest on sandy sea floors, as every fish, octopus and crab in the area will hone in on the wreck, like it was an oasis in a sea of sand.

In the following pages we will explore the famous, not-so-famous and some very unusual shipwrecks from around the world. Most of these shipwrecks are in depths that only scuba divers can reach, but a few of the shallow ones can be enjoyed by snorkelers of any age. So let's explore shipwrecks.

MV Union Star 17

One of Malaysia's most spectacular shipwrecks is the *MV Union Star 17*, or as it is known locally 'the Sugar Wreck'. This 90m (295ft) long freighter sank off the east coast of Malaysia as a result of a leak in the hull in December 2000. Fortunately the captain and 16 crewmembers were able to safely abandon the sinking ship without loss of life. At the time of sinking, the ship was loaded with a cargo of sugar, hence the popular name. The ship's cargo has long since dissolved, but laying on its starboard side in only 19m (62 ft) of water, the *MV Union Star 17* remains extremely popular with both fish and divers.

Millions of fish love this shipwreck as it is the only shelter in a vast area of sand. Dense schools of fish swarm all over the ship, and also swim in the cargo holds that were once full of sugar. Divers also love this shipwreck because of all the fish life, and also because the ship is almost intact, with all its fittings in place. It is very unusual to explore a shipwreck with all its portholes, lights, winches, shackles and ropes still in place, as they are usually salvaged or stolen. The *MV Union Star 17* is one of the sweetest shipwrecks that divers can explore in Asia.

Aarhus

Off the coast of Brisbane, Australia, is a notorious rocky reef known as Smith Rock. Over the years this treacherous rock has claimed three ships, including the historic *Aarhus*.

The *Aarhus* was a 52m (170ft) long steel hull sailing ship with three masts and classic good looks. The ship was built in Hamburg, Germany, in 1875 and carried cargo in voyages around the world.

On 24 February 1894, the *Aarhus* was sailing into Brisbane after a long journey from New York, USA, when the vessel suddenly encountered Smith Rock. The rock ripped a hole in the ship's hull that caused it to sink very quickly, but not before the Captain and crew of 13 were able to safely abandon ship.

The *Aarhus* was not rediscovered until 1979 and today is protected as a historic shipwreck. The wreck is very broken up and spread over the sandy sea floor at a depth of 21m (69ft). It is also a home to gropers, stingrays, wobbegong sharks and lots of fish. But divers still get a lot of enjoyment exploring the ribs, masts, hull plating and inspecting the cargo which included rolls of barb wire. Every visit to the *Aarhus* is different, as storms regularly shift the sand about to uncover different parts of this historic shipwreck.

29

SS Yongala

Australia's most famous shipwreck is rated as one of the best dive sites in the world, but years ago, the *SS Yongala* was more famous as a ghost ship.

The *SS Yongala* was built for the Adelaide Steamship Company in 1903 and was named after a town in South Australia of the same name. Designed to carry passengers and cargo, the vessel was a 109m (357ft) long steam ship.

On 14 March 1911 the *SS Yongala* departed Melbourne on its 99th and final voyage, to Cairns in North Queensland. After stops in Brisbane and Mackay, the *SS Yongala* was south of Townsville when it ran straight into a fierce cyclone. The ship didn't stand a chance and sank quickly on March 24, 1911, tragically taking all 124 passengers and crew to a watery grave.

The *SS Yongala's* disappearance caused quite a stir and a large scale search was undertaken to find the ship and any survivors. However the search proved fruitless. Minor wreckage was later found washed ashore along the nearby coastline, but the only body ever found was that of a racehorse, called Moonshine, that was being transported on the *SS Yongala*.

Years after the *SS Yongala* disappeared locals reported seeing a ship, matching the size and description of the lost ship. The *SS Yongala* was sailing again as a ghost ship.

Then, in 1943, a minesweeper discovered a large object 12 nautical miles off Cape Bowling Green. The object was thought to be a ship, but wasn't confirmed until divers explored the site in 1958 and discovered that it was in fact the long lost *SS Yongala*.

Today the *SS Yongala* is rated as one of the best shipwreck dives in the world. The ship rests on its starboard side in 29m (95ft) and is mostly intact, but is also a very spectacular artificial reef and a haven for marine life. The fish life that populates the *SS Yongala* is unbelievable; massive schools of barracuda, trevally, sweetlips, snapper, gropers and much more. But divers also encounter turtles, rays, sharks and sea snakes on this famous shipwreck.

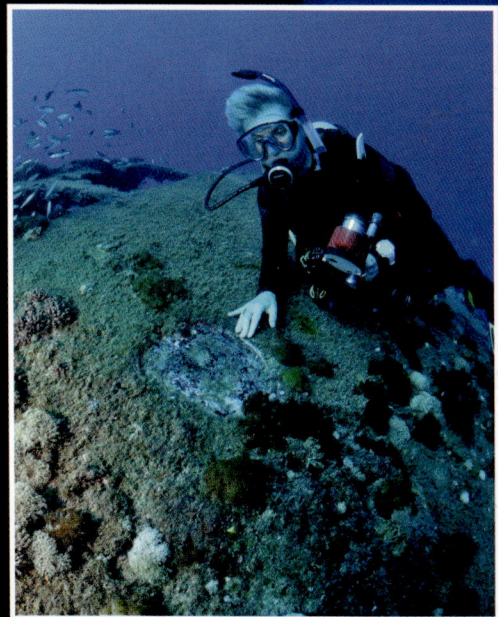

USAT Liberty

The *USAT Liberty* has the unique distinction of being wounded by a torpedo before finally being sunk by a volcano, 20 years later.

Built in 1918, the 125m (410ft) long *USAT Liberty* was a cargo ship that went straight into service in World War I for the United States Navy. The ship carried horses and other cargo from America to France to help with the war effort.

After the war, the *USAT Liberty* went into service as a general cargo ship, but when America jointed World War II in 1941, the ship returned to military service.

On 11 January 1942, the *USAT Liberty* was on a voyage from Australia to the Philippines when it was torpedoed by a Japanese submarine off the coast of Bali, Indonesia. The ship miraculously stayed afloat, but later while being towed to a nearby port it started to sink. The ship was run aground on Bali, at a town called Tulamben, so its cargo could be removed.

The ship remained high and dry on the beach at Tulamben until 1963 when a nearby volcano erupted. The violent shaking of the earth by the volcano caused the *USAT Liberty* to slide off the beach and settle underwater.

Today the *USAT Liberty* is the most famous shipwreck in Indonesia and visited by many tourists to Bali. The shipwreck is broken up in parts, but still a great dive in depths from 5m to 35m (16–114ft). The shallow sections of the wreck can be explored by snorkelers, and are often engulfed in a large school of trevally. While it is fun to get inside the shipwreck, the corals and masses of fish make the *USAT Liberty* such a wonderful shipwreck to visit.

Scottish Prince

Very few ships sink with a cargo of treasure, but treasure comes in many different forms, as the locals of the Gold Coast in Queensland, Australia found when the *Scottish Prince* sank with a cargo of whisky and beer.

The *Scottish Prince* was a 64m (210ft) long steel hull barque sailing ship that transported cargo between Scotland and Australia. On 3 February, 1887 the ship was off the Gold Coast, Australia, when it ran aground late at night.

News of the grounding quickly spread, especially when it was discovered that the *Scottish Prince* was carrying a cargo of beer and whisky. Before the ship and its cargo could be salvaged some enterprising locals visited the ship and helped themselves to its precious cargo, which probably led to some wild parties and very sore heads.

Before all the cargo could be liberated the ship sank in stormy weather and was then forgotten until divers rediscovered the *Scottish Prince* in 1954, resting in 12m (39ft) of water. The divers also discovered that much of its cargo was undamaged, with hundreds of whisky bottles buried in the sand.

Today the *Scottish Prince* is a wonderful shipwreck to explore and always swarming with fish life. The ship is broken up and full of sand, but the bow and stern sections are still quite distinguishable. Schools of yellowtail often cover the entire shipwreck, but the wreck is also home to gropers, wobbegong sharks, moray eels, octopus, rays and reef fish. And every now and then another old whisky bottle is uncovered on this fascinating shipwreck.

SS President Coolidge

Built in 1931, the 198m (650ft) long *SS President Coolidge* was an ocean liner and the largest merchant ship built in America at the time. The ship was considered luxury afloat, decked out with the finest of fittings and carried passengers on voyages from San Francisco to ports across Asia.

After America entered World War II in 1941 the *SS President Coolidge* was converted to carry troops and cargo. Her luxury fittings were either removed or covered up, and additional toilets and bunk beds were added to accommodate the troops.

In October 1942, the ship was transporting over 5000 American troops to a base on the island of Espirtu Santo, Vanuatu, when disaster struck. Entering the harbor at Luganville the crew of the *SS President Coolidge* were unaware that they were entering a minefield. The ship hit two mines and started taking on water. The captain ordered the *SS President Coolidge* to be run aground before it sank.

With the ship sitting precariously on a sloping beach, nets and ladders were dropped, lifeboats lowered and the troops abandoned the sinking ship. The troops left everything – rifles, helmets and personal gear. Only 74 minutes after striking the first mine the *SS President Coolidge* disappeared below the waves. Remarkably, only two men died.

Today the *SS President Coolidge* is one of the most spectacular shipwrecks in the world. The ship is accessible from the shore and lies on its starboard side in depths between 20m and 70m (65–230ft). A fascinating ship to explore, divers can enter its cargo holds where jeeps, trucks, fuel tanks, munitions and other equipment can be seen. Rifles and helmets still litter its decks, dropped by the troops as they abandoned ship.

It takes many dives to explore this huge shipwreck. Divers tour the engine room, cargo holds, cabins, dining room, barber shop and even the swimming pool. Rows of toilets can be seen, as can the captain's private bathroom. The most famous object on the ship, the sculpture of a lady and unicorn, is located in the first class smoking room. A remarkable relic on a remarkable shipwreck.

HMAS Swan

Over the last 20 years a number of retired Royal Australian Navy ships have been given a new life as artificial reefs, scuttled in the seas around Australia. The very first of these ships to be sunk was *HMAS Swan* in 1997.

Launched in 1967, *HMAS Swan* was a 113m (370ft) long River Class Destroyer Escort. During the ship's operational life it served around Australia and throughout Asia and the Pacific, often involved in humanitarian work.

HMAS Swan was decommissioned in 1996 and unlike all previous Navy warships, which were sold for scrap metal, the ship was gifted to the government of Western Australia. They decided the best use of the ship was as an artificial reef, to attract divers to the state, and a site was chosen off Dunsborough, south of Perth.

A year was spent cleaning and preparing the vessel, before the ship was towed to its final resting place. On 14 December 1997, Australia got its first warship artificial reef when a series of explosions sent *HMAS Swan* to the bottom, leaving it sitting upright on its keel in 30m (98ft) of water.

Today *HMAS Swan* is a spectacular dive site and a success story for the creation of artificial reefs. People now come from all around the world to explore this wonderful shipwreck. Divers can explore almost every part of the ship, as many access holes have been cut through the hull. But the bridge is a very popular spot for photos, with divers lining up to sit in the Captain's chair.

In the time *HMAS Swan* has been on the ocean floor it has become covered in sponges and other pretty growth. Divers exploring this wreck are always amazed by the amount of fish and other marine life that live on this old warship.

Tangalooma Wrecks

In the past, when ships outlived their working lives they were either sold for scrap metal or scuttled in deep water. But occasionally, old ships were also used to create break walls, like the Tangalooma Wrecks.

Located on the western side of Moreton Island in Brisbane, Australia, the Tangalooma Wrecks is made up of 15 vessels scuttled to form a shelter for small boats. The ships were sunk, end to end, in 1963, and are old bucket dredges, suction dredges and barges.

Today the ships sit in depths from 2m to 10m (6–32ft), and while a fair portion of the ships stick out above the surface, what lies beneath makes for a fascinating snorkelling and diving site.

Corals grow profusely on these wrecks, and tropical fish abound, making the site like a giant aquarium. Divers often encounter turtles and wobbegong sharks, but the most unusual thing people see on the Tangalooma Wrecks are birds, underwater! Shags roost on top of these wrecks and hunt around them for fish, and they are so used to people that they just swim around them.

HMAS Brisbane

On 31 July 2005, a series of explosions off Queensland's Sunshine Coast created Australia's newest dive site when an old warship was scuttled. That ship was the *HMAS Brisbane*, a 133m (436ft) long guided missile destroyer, that is today one of the most popular dive sites in Australia.

HMAS Brisbane was built in America and commissioned into the Royal Australia Navy in 1967. The ship had a crew of 307 men and was a very swift ship, with a top speed of 35 knots, which earned it the nickname 'the steel cat'.

HMAS Brisbane had a very distinguished career, and served in war zones in Vietnam and the Persian Gulf. After being decommissioned in 2001 the future of the ship was put out to tender, with a group called the Sunshine Coast Artificial Reef Group winning the tender with their plan to sink the ship as a dive tourist attraction.

Today the *HMAS Brisbane* rests in 27m (90ft) of water off Mooloolaba and is a very exciting dive site. Divers can explore all parts of the ship – the engine room, galley, and control room being some of the highlights. But a favourite stop off point for all divers is the two big five inch guns that sit on its forward and rear decks.

Within weeks of being scuttled fish had discovered *HMAS Brisbane*, and today thousands of reef and pelagic fish swarm around this wonderful old warship.

MV Dona Marilyn

The Philippines is a nation of over 7,000 islands, and as such the most convenient way for most people to travel around the country is by ferry. Inter-island ferries operate across the nation, and the 98m (289ft) long *MV Dona Marilyn* was one that operated between Manila and Cebu.

On 24 October 1988, the *MV Dona Marilyn* was off the coast of Cebu when it was caught in a dreadful typhoon. The ship sank in the horrible conditions. It was a terrible tragedy, with 389 people dying and only 147 surviving the sinking.

The shipwreck of the *MV Dona Marilyn* now lies on its starboard side in 33m (108ft) of water. Today it is a fitting tribute to those that perished, as the ship has been transformed into a spectacular artificial reef. Covering the ship are beautiful black coral trees and gorgeous soft corals, making the shipwreck stunning to look at. The wreck is also home to a diverse range of reef fish, plus stingrays, eagle rays and reef sharks.

The *MV Dona Marilyn* is such a huge shipwreck that it takes quite a few dives to see all the features of the ship. The ship is mostly intact and divers can see its masts, bridge, numerous cabins and other features of this immense shipwreck.

SS Francis Preston Blair

The Coral Sea Reefs, beyond Australia's famous Great Barrier Reef, have claimed many ships over the last few centuries. Most of these ships were smashed to pieces on these rugged coral reefs, but there is one that can still be seen quite clearly, the *SS Francis Preston Blair*.

Built in 1943, the 140m (459ft) long *SS Francis Preston Blair* was an American Liberty ship, a type of cargo ship that was mass produced during World War II in America.

On 15 July 1945, the *SS Francis Preston Blair* was steaming off Saumarez Reef, some 300km (186 miles) off the coastline of Queensland, Australia, when it ended up on top of the reef. There are a number of stories about how the ship ended up in that unique position, including the strange tale of a cyclone, a very rare event at that time of year.

The most commonly believed story is that the ship was being stalked by a Japanese submarine, and fearing that they would be torpedoed and sink in deep water, the Captain decided to run the ship onto the reef instead.

Today the *SS Francis Preston Blair* still sits high, and mostly dry, on top of the reef and is in remarkable condition considering it has been exposed to the elements and several real cyclones. It also survived being used for target practise by the Royal Australian Air Force that dropped numerous practise bombs on the shipwreck in the 1980s.

The ship today is home to hundreds of sea birds and is one of the largest shipwrecks sitting on land in Australia. Unfortunately, Saumarez Reef is a long way from anywhere, so the *SS Francis Preston Blair* rarely gets explored.

Cementco

One of the most unusual shipwrecks in Australia is called the *Cementco*, and known locally as the upside down shipwreck!

Built in 1944 for the Australian Army, the *Cementco* was originally named the *Crusader*, and was a 67m (220ft) long barge designed to transport tanks and other heavy equipment. During World War II the ship did two trips from Australia to Papua New Guinea carrying equipment and supplies to Australian troops.

After the war, the ship was sold, renamed and remodeled to carry dead coral that had been dredged off Brisbane. For 40 years the ship carried loads of coral to be turned into cement.

When the *Cementco* was too old to work, a local Brisbane dive club got hold of the ship and planned to sink it as an artificial reef. Whilst being towed off Brisbane's Moreton Island the ship never reached its final resting place as rough seas swamped the vessel and it sank prematurely on 27 July 1985. The *Cementco* ended up on a rocky reef at 25m (82ft) and in an upside down position!

Today the *Cementco* is a very interesting shipwreck to see, as it is rare to find an upside down ship. The shipwreck doesn't look like a traditional ship or shipwreck, more like a giant metal box. However, it is still fascinating to explore as the wreck is home to countless reef fish.

HTMS Sattakut

Not many ships have such a long and varied career as the *HTMS Sattakut*.

Built in 1944 for the United States Navy, the HTMS Sattakut was a 48m (157ft) long landing craft infantry, designed to carry troops and land them directly onto beaches. There were so many of these ships built that they were not given names. This one was simply called *USS LCI (M) 739*. The vessel and its crew served in the Pacific at the end of World War II and landed troops at famous battle sites in Palau, Iwo Jima and Okinawa.

After the war, the vessel was commissioned into the Royal Thai Navy and in 1947, was renamed. In 2007, the *HTMS Sattakut* was finally retired, striped and cleaned in preparation for a new life as an artificial reef.

On 18 June 2011, the vessel was scuttled at its finally resting place, off the island of Koh Tao, Thailand. But things didn't quite go to plan. The ship rolled on its side and ended up in that position on the sea floor. Two months later a salvage team lifted the ship, rotated it and positioned it back on the bottom, this time sitting upright on its keel.

Today the *HTMS Sattakut* is a wonderful shipwreck to explore, sitting on a sandy sea floor 30m (98ft) deep. The ship is compact but has a lot to offer, with divers able to explore the bridge area and admire its deck guns. In the short time it has been underwater the *HTMS Sattakut* has attracted a wealth of fish species, including many gropers.

Taiyo

When most ships sink they end up lying on their keel or side, but occasionally they end up in a completely unexpected position, like the *Taiyo* shipwreck.

Not a lot of background information is known about this mysterious shipwreck in the Solomon Islands, but it has become a very popular dive site near the island of Uepi. Rumor has it that on its maiden voyage, just over a decade ago, the crew of the 33m (108ft) long *Taiyo* fishing boat were so busy celebrating that they didn't notice a reef until they ran into it!

The brand new *Taiyo* ended up sitting on the reef. Attempts were made to salvage and refloat the ship, but they went disastrously wrong. The ship slipped off the reef and sunk, ending up sitting precariously on a ledge in a vertical position!

How the *Taiyo* didn't disappear into deep water is a puzzle, but somehow the stern of the ship landed on the only ledge on a vertical wall of coral. The ship today is an amazing sight, sitting perfectly vertical with the bow in 3m (10ft) and the stern in 36m (118ft). The ship still has all its fittings, but coral and fish now populate this very unique shipwreck.

USS Tucker

The *USS Tucker* was an American destroyer built in 1936. The 104m (341ft) long ship was part of the United States Battle Fleet. It was berthed at Pearl Harbor, Hawaii, on 7 December 1941 when it was attacked by the Imperial Japanese Navy. Many ships were sunk in the surprise attack, but the *USS Tucker* was lucky to escape with little damage.

The *USS Tucker* went on to serve in the Pacific Ocean throughout World War II and on 4 August 1942, and was escorting a supply ship to Espiritu Santo, Vanuatu, when disaster struck. The USS Tucker ran into an underwater mine and the explosion from the mine was so great that it snapped the ship in two, causing it to sink very quickly. Three men were killed by the explosion, but the rest of the crew managed to evacuate the ship safely. The most unfortunate part of the whole incident was that it was an American mine, that had only been laid the day before, which ultimately sunk the ship.

Today the *USS Tucker* is broken up in depths between 15m and 18m (49–59ft). One of the reasons the ship is so broken up is that not long after the ship sunk, an American pilot dropped bombs on the wreck mistakenly thinking it was a Japanese submarine. When exploring the wreck, parts of the destroyer are easy to identify, like the stern, bow, engine and drive shaft, but the rest of the ship looks like a pile of twisted metal. The *USS Tucker* is still a wonderful shipwreck to explore, and a good place to see turtles, gropers and a wide variety of reef fish.

MV Pacific Gas

During World War II a number of ships were sunk around Papua New Guinea in fierce battles. Some of these shipwrecks are spectacular, but surprisingly, one of the most popular shipwrecks, called the *MV Pacific Gas,* in Papua New Guinea was sunk well after the war.

Built in Japan in 1967, the 65m (213ft) long liquefied gas carrier was originally called the *MS Nanayo Maru*. But after being purchased by an Australian company in 1972 the ship was renamed the *MV Pacific Gas*. For the next eight years the ship transported gas between Australia and Papua New Guinea until it was retired out of service in 1980.

Sitting unused in the harbor at Port Moresby for many years, the ship started to deteriorate from neglect. By 1986 it was in such a bad state that the Harbor Master said the ship had to go. At this stage a local diver stepped in and offered to sink the ship as an artificial reef, joining a number of other vessels scuttled in the area. The owners were happy to agree.

After being cleaned and having its huge gas tank removed the *MV Pacific Gas* was scuttled off Port Moresby on 15 October 1986. The ship now rests on a sandy slope in depths from 20m to 45m (65–148ft) and is a wonderful shipwreck to explore. The wreck is covered in pretty corals and is home to countless fish. Divers can explore the hold, bridge and other parts of the shipwreck.

While the *MV Pacific Gas* is great to dive during the day, it is extra special at night. Divers descend on the bow after dark, arrange themselves around a hatch and then turn off their torches. This may sound very creepy, and it is. But your eyes quickly adjust, especially when you see hundreds of green lights flickering inside the hatch. These are flashlight fish, which have a luminous organ under their eye to help them find food at night. Suddenly the fish emerge from the hatch and thousands of fairy lights spread across the ship, lighting it up like a Christmas tree. Truly a spectacular sight to see.

Azusa Maru

During World War II so many ships were sunk by planes, mines and other ships that the full histories of these shipwrecks are yet to fully be discovered. One such ship is the *Azusa Maru*.

Little is really known about the 50m (164ft) long freighter, the *Azusa Maru*, and even if that is its correct name. What is known is that the ship now rests in 40m (131ft) of water in the Solomon Islands, at a remote location called Wickham Harbor.

Wickham Harbor was used by the Japanese as a base during World War II. In 1942, American planes bombed the base and the ships that were anchored in the harbor. At least four ships were sunk, including the *Azusa Maru*, and all are wonderful shipwrecks to explore.

The *Azusa Maru* is a compact shipwreck. Unlike most of the shipwrecks in this area it was not salvaged after the war, so it is virtually intact. Divers can explore the cargo holds, which contain artillery guns, munitions and other equipment. One of the main features of this shipwreck is the mast, which still has a brass lantern in place which is now covered in coral. Typical of all shipwrecks the *Azusa Maru* is a haven for fish and is also visited by reef sharks.

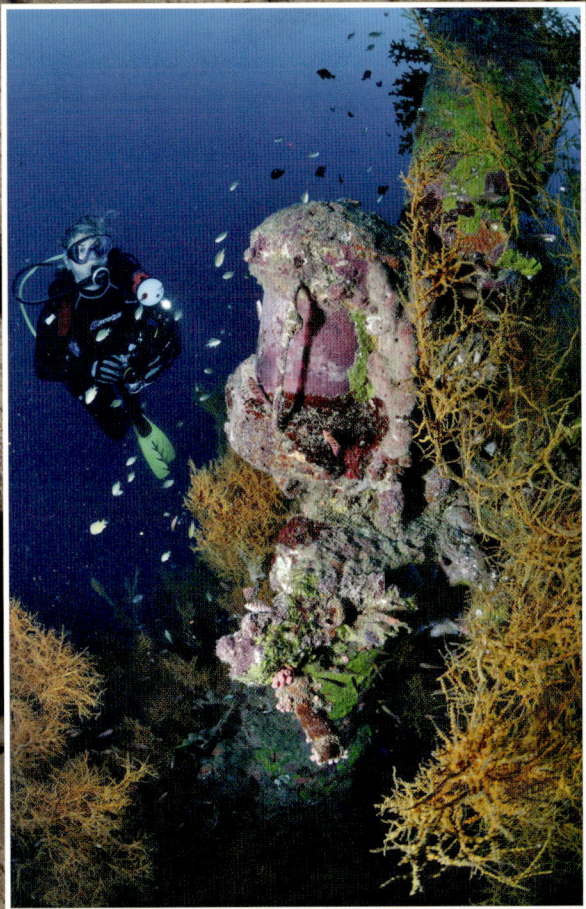

Other Wrecks

Ships are not the only manmade objects that end up on the bottom of the ocean, as planes, cars, trucks and even tanks end up in the sea.

While not as big as shipwrecks, plane wrecks are always fascinating to explore. The great majority of plane wrecks that can now be seen underwater are a result of World War II, with plane wrecks on show in Papua New Guinea and Solomon Islands in particular.

Most cars, trucks and tanks that end up underwater have generally fallen off ships. However, at the end of World War II the Americans dumped many heavy vehicles into the sea around the South Pacific, rather than take them back to the USA or give them to the locals. One of these famous dumping sites is called Million Dollar Point, at Espiritu Santo, Vanuatu, where today cranes, trucks and other vehicles can be seen in depths from 5m to 50m (16–164ft). Million Dollar Point is a reminder of the wastes of war.

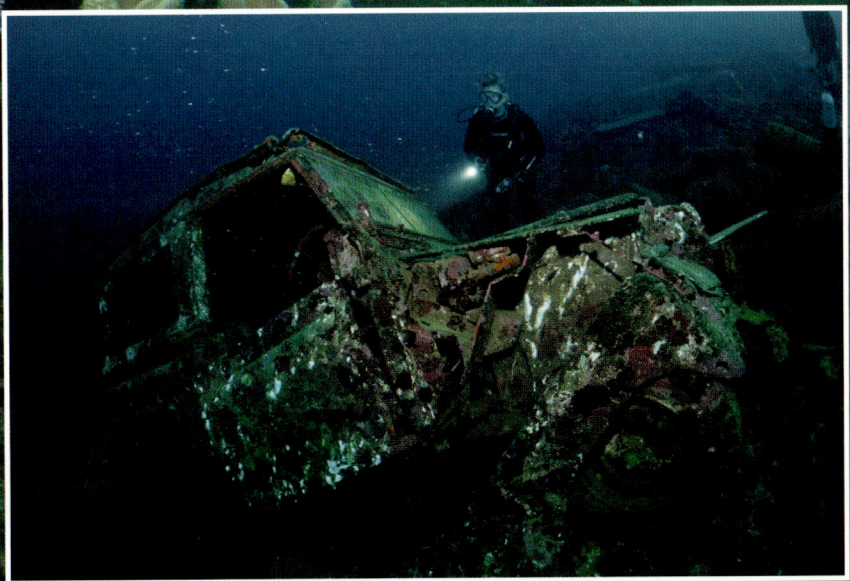

Glossary

BARQUE – A type of sailing ship with three or more masts.

BOW – The front of a ship.

PORT – The left side of a ship.

ECOSYSTEM – A community of animals and plants that live side by side.

GPS – Global Positioning System, using satellites to pinpoint a location.

INVERTEBRATE – An animal without a backbone.

KEEL – The bottom section of a ship.

MOLLUSCS – A group of soft bodied animals that usually live in a shell, like snails.

MUNITIONS – Material used in war, such as ammunition.

RADAR – A device that uses radio waves to detect objects at a distance.

SCUBA – Self Contained Underwater Breathing Apparatus, used by divers to explore the oceans.

STARBOARD – The right side of a ship.

STERN – The back of a ship.

First published in 2016 by New Holland Publishers Pty Ltd
London • Sydney • Auckland

The Chandlery Unit 704 50 Westminster Bridge Road London SE1 7QY United Kingdom
1/66 Gibbes Street Chatswood NSW 2067 Australia
5/39 Woodside Ave Northcote, Auckland 0627 New Zealand

www.newhollandpublishers.com

A record of this book is held at the British Library and the National Library of Australia.

ISBN 9781921580178

Managing Director: Fiona Schultz
Publisher: Diane Ward
Project Editor: Jessica McNamara
Designer: Peter Guo
Production Director: Olga Dementiev
Printer: Toppan Leefung Printing Limited

10 9 8 7 6 5 4 3 2 1

Keep up with New Holland Publishers on Facebook
www.facebook.com/NewHollandPublishers